30 MORE DAYS WITH JESUS

By: Bernadette Hanson

Bloomingdale, Illinois

Copyright © 2011

Bernadette Hanson for McClure Publishing, Inc.

All rights reserved. Printed and bound in the United States of America. According to the 1976 United States Copyright Act, no part of this book may be reproduced or utilized in any form or by any means, electronic or mechanical, including photocopying, recording, or by any information storage or retrieval system, except by a reviewer who may quote brief passages in a review to be printed in a magazine or newspaper, without permission in writing from the Publisher: Inquiries should be addressed to McClure Publishing, Inc. Permissions Department, 358 West Army Trail Road, #205, Bloomingdale, IL 60108. First Printing: March, 2011.

Unless otherwise indicated, all scriptural quotations are from the King James Version (KJV) of the Bible. All references to satan are purposely lower cased, because we give no credit to satan.

Ellipses in this book indicate where you should pause and think before proceeding.

The author and publisher have made every effort to ensure the accuracy and completeness of information contained in this book. We assume no responsibility for errors, inaccuracies, omissions, or any inconsistency therein.

Any slights of people, places, belief systems or organizations are unintentional. Any resemblance to anyone living, dead or somewhere in between is truly coincidental.

ISBN-13: **978-0983369707**

ISBN-10: 0-9833697-0-4

LCCN: 2011925788

Book design by McClure Publishing, Inc.

To order additional copies, please contact:
McClure Publishing, Inc.
www.mcclurepublishing.com
800.659.4908
mcclurepublishing@msn.com

Invitation

Precious Brother and Sister,

It is no accident that you are reading this book. The Lord has made a way for you to receive this urgent invitation.

Please look into your heart, right now, and make a decision to receive the Lord, Jesus, as your personal Lord, Messiah, and Saviour. Admit that you have sinned, as the Word of God tells us that we all have sinned and fallen short of the glory of God, Romans 3:23.

Repent of your sin against God, Acts 3:19, and confess with your mouth the Lord Jesus and believe in your heart that God raised Him from the dead, Romans 10:9.

If you have said this prayer and believed it with your heart, you are born again. May I, be the first to welcome you to your new heavenly family. I urge you to attend the Christian church that the Lord Jesus guides you to.

You are about to embark on the greatest adventure of your life.

Welcome home,

b

Dedication

This work is lovingly dedicated to my Lord and Saviour, Jesus Christ.

Without You, I am nothing. I praise and thank You, Lord for Your ever keeping power, for your unspeakable gift of forgiveness, for Your mercy, Your grace, Your kindness, and Your all encompassing agape love.

Thank You, Lord, for never giving up on me and for the many wonderful people You have placed across my path in this life, the many mentors, and the wonderful, supportive friends, family, and Christian brothers and sisters you have blessed me with.

You are everything to me, My Lord.

I love You,

b

Introduction

Beloved Reader,

For each one that enjoyed the first book of this series, "30 Days with Jesus", and was greatly blessed by it, now comes the second book, "30 More Days with Jesus". This book not only picks up where the other one left off, but also includes the original 30 days as a prelude.

You are about to read a most unusual book. The Lord, Jesus, came to wake me up in the early morning hours to speak about things that have already happened, things that are yet to come, and things of heaven and of hell. This began in 2007 and continues to this day.

I urge you, if you have not already done so, to pray the prayer you will find at the beginning of this book, to receive the Lord Jesus into your heart.

You will receive and understand so much more from what the Lord desires to show you from this wonderful work He has done when your spirit man has been born again.

I speak a blessing into your life and I pray that as you read this book, the Lord will speak to your heart, bless your soul and reveal things to you that bring comfort and peace.

Your Sister in Christ Jesus,

b

Contents

PRELUDE - FIRST 30 DAYS WITH JESUS 11
Day 1 13
Day 2 15
Day 3 17
Day 4 19
Day 5 21
Day 6 23
Day 7 25
Day 8 27
Day 9 29
Day 10 31
Day 11 33
Day 12 35
Day 13 37
Day 14 39
Day 15 41
Day 16 43
Day 17 45
Day 18 47
Day 19 49
Day 20 51
Day 21 53
Day 22 55
Day 23 57
Day 24 59

Day 25..61

Day 26..63

Day 27..65

Day 28..67

Day 29..69

Day 30..71

Revelation of the Front Cover..75

30 MORE DAYS WITH JESUS...77

Day 31..79

Day 32..81

Day 33..83

Day 34..84

Day 35..85

Day 36..86

Day 37..87

Day 38..89

Day 39..91

Day 40..93

Day 41..95

Day 42..97

Day 43..99

Day 44..101

Day 45..103

Day 46..105

Day 47..107

Day 48..109

Day 49..111

Day 50	113
Day 51	115
Day 52	117
Day 53	119
Day 54	121
Day 55	123
Day 56	125
Day 57	127
Day 58	129
Day 59	131
Day 60	133
BONUS DAY	135

There are scripture references for each day from Day 1 to Day 60. Please read these daily devotionals along with referencing your Bible.

PRELUDE

FIRST 30 DAYS WITH JESUS

Day 1

{Ephesians 4:26}

Anger is always a no win situation. I know you go through aggravating situations, but anger can only lead to sin and sin leads to death.

Have you read in My word ... be angry and sin not ... take not your own revenge ... bless those that curse you ... pray for those that despitefully use you?

Anger also leads to sickness. Some of My own children are suffering sickness because of their anger. Agree with your enemy quickly, loose and release them to Me, overcome evil with good.

To walk in constant forgiveness is to walk in constant health. Righteous anger is meant to correct a wrong, (such as the money changers in the temple). When Jesus walked this earth, there were many that came against Him, He prayed and set a consistent quiet time with Me to loose and release His cares.

Truly, you must give your cares to Me. I will make right what your enemies do to you. I see all, I know all, and yes, I am merciful to your enemies ... to a point. If they do not repent, they will reap the harvest born of hurting you ... not only that, but they will see My unlimited favor upon you. The more they attack, the more favor I will release.

Forgiveness is the key to having your enemies walk in peace with you. The physical body is meant to only carry a healthy amount of stress ... a level that motivates you to action ... but not so much that it makes you sick physically.

My people are under great stress right now and I hear their groaning ... just as when they were in Egypt ... and now just as then I will bring them out.

Day 2

{Jeremiah 29:11}

Child, there are many things I want you to know. First, that My love is perfect and everlasting ... that My mercy and grace truly are new for you every morning ... that you mean so much to Me.

I will take you in some unusual and strange paths. There are some places and some people that only you can reach. I always prepare you before I send you. When you begin your ministry you will be well equipped ... you will be able to completely trust Me.

I will temper (prepare) you in fiery trials first. You will learn to deal with attitudes and situations, first. I will humble you before I elevate you. I will allow hurts and disappointments to get you ready to be in the habit of turning to Me first.

I will repeat and repeat painful experiences until you learn My way to deal with them. This is why some are stuck at different levels of their training (preparations) ... they do not allow Me to do the work I need to in order to prepare them for the ministry I created them for.

Each one has a plan and a purpose. Every vessel has an anointing and a measure of faith. Faith grows through trials ... humility through disappointments. I will never allow frustration to the point of breaking one's spirit, but I do allow tempering to reach the final goal.

Stubbornness and anger only put you back into training. Submission and repentance allow you to move onwards. Submit quickly ... move up to the next level quickly.

Can anyone fight My will? My purpose? (like a fish struggling in a net) It is useless and will only exhaust you.

Trust and submission ... this is pleasing to Me.

Day 3

{Isaiah 40:31}

*E*xpect something wonderful ... so many of Mine expect bad things to happen ... they receive and believe bad reports from doctors ... they don't expect promotion or provision or prosperity and all these things have already been promised and paid for.

Redemption not only bought back souls, but all things needed in this earthly realm. I know you have need of money, shelter, clothing, and cars. I have provided for this. You have not because you receive not.

If you ask me ... it's My pleasure to give ... My great pleasure. But remember, it will be according to My perfect timing. I will not leave ... I will not forsake ... I will not withhold what is needful to My children. They are blessed in all the earth.

I am still protecting and providing as I did for the Israelites in the desert ... a cloud by day and a pillar of fire by night. My children are impatient. They want to lead and direct me—NOT SO. Those who wait upon Me shall mount up as eagle's wings. Wait, I say, wait upon the Lord.

Blessings have been missed because My people won't wait ... they settle for less than I intended for them. Have I not said ... NEVER the less? My people should stand out ...

be prosperous, healthy, and wise ... they are My representatives. But instead, they are poor, blind, and naked.

When will you learn ... when will you listen ... when will you wait upon Me? I long to bless My children, but I will not throw pearls before swine. WAIT patiently and gain wisdom.

Day 4

{Acts 2:17}

It's true, these are the days I will pour out My Spirit upon all men ... all who believe in Me and call out and follow Me. Gifts of Healing and Deliverance and Prophesy will flow as never before.

My people will be warned and corrected as never before. Things have been loosed in the earth---evil things---that the world has never seen ... but My strength and My power has also been released as never before.

Those who have an ear to hear Me will make it through the coming disasters. Many will lose hope and give up. I am always near ... as near as your next heartbeat, but some will miss Me, My warnings, and My power anyway. You must spend time with Me in order to know My voice.

The enemy is subtle; he will mix scripture with truth. Have I not said that the end time is cut off early so the very elect will not fall? (Matthew 24:22) My sheep must know My voice for there are wolves in sheep's clothing just waiting to lead them astray.

Beware of "new" revelations of My Word that don't line up with it. My Word confirms itself. I have made your spirit man to receive a check when things do not agree with or line up with My Word.

Bernadette Hanson

You must draw nigh to Me as never before. Dangers and temptations abound. It's becoming worse than the days of Noah ... one of the biggest deceptions is that you are safe because I delay My coming.

My true servants will be mocked and persecuted for their fervent pleas to repent and return to Me. Believe Me, the time is very short now and My Word must come to pass.

I will that none should perish ... hell is real ... but each one has free will to choose their eternal resting place.

Day 5

{I John 1:4}

*J*oy and anger cannot abide in the same place at the same time. Anger is detrimental to your health ... spirit, soul, and body. It leads to hatred which leads to sin (murder).

You can have joy in spite of your circumstances ... you can have peace in a storm (calm) ... this is much different from happiness ... which depends on what's going on.

I will that My people have joy that is full and complete. In the midst of trials I will send joy unspeakable to help you bear through it. Joy gives strength ... it has healing properties ... like a bubbling fountain on the inside that cannot be stopped.

Joy is a replenisher while anger saps all your energy. One heals ... one destroys. I would that My people be full of joy at all times. They need only ask. Joy is something desperately needed in theses times.

Another replenisher is speaking in tongues ... and it is a (spiritual) weapon ... a way for our spirits to commune on a deeper level ... a way to come into My presence. Tongues are for this time, when demonic attacks are great ... there is a much greater need to be in My presence.

Bernadette Hanson

Darkness and light cannot occupy the same space and when you are in My presence ... you are in the light. Darkness understands it not ... confuse the enemy by coming into My presence in the midst of your trials. Anger will try to have you blame Me and be separated ... but this is when you need Me the most.

Many turn away from Me in trials when this is the very thing intended to bring them closer to Me ... to show others where strength can be found and renewed.

Day 6

{I Peter 5:8}

To be sure, the devil is moving, but remember where sin and evil abounds, My grace abounds more. My grace is the strength you need to fight the enemy. My way will be done; there is no way to stop My plan.

Everything has been orchestrated. Even the evil that is now in the world ... I have planned it. This is the time for the greatest outpouring of My Spirit on earth. Miracles that have not been seen since the time of the book of Acts will happen and are happening even now.

Yet in the midst of even these, the faith of some will wax cold. Many will give up on the miracles they've been praying and waiting for just as they are about to happen because of discouragement and impatience.

I will reign miracles on the just and the unjust to verify to all that I alone am the Lord and there is none like Me. Some will choose to not believe even when a miracle happens right in front of them.

They will reason and attribute it to luck, chance, etc. Even now, I am moving in the earth as never before. Many will come to know Me and be saved. Never doubt that hell is a real place ... a place of pain and torment ... a place of darkness devoid of My presence.

The angels that fell are full of hate and violence and take joy in their torture of lost souls. Truly, hell does enlarge herself by the day. The torments there are as indescribable as the joys of heaven.

I grieve for every soul that denies Me and chooses to go in the opposite direction. At the same time, there is great joy for each one that chooses to believe in Me.

Day 7

{James 1:19}

Divine protection is given to those who will listen and wait. I will protect the impatient, but not to the same degree.

My Word says to be slow to speak ... not to do. Blessings are for those who obey quickly. I know My requests may sometimes seem strange, but My ways are not your ways.

Jesus heard and obeyed and that's what I expect of My people. Remember that I am coming soon. I look upon men's hearts ... I know their real motives and intentions. The Father has angels that record such things.

Many do the right things with hearts full of deceit ... wanting man to see and glorify them, while others will silently endure hardship after hardship and only I know what they're going through ... these will be blessed by Me.

Remember that human appreciation is very fickle ... here today; gone tomorrow ... that is why it is better to obey God than man. Even Jesus got cheers one day (riding in on a donkey) and jeers and insults the next (going to the cross ... "crucify Him").

The crucifixion was the most cruel, painful, slowest way to die that man had. Jesus endured every type of abuse and shame, and yet obeyed. Some of Mine have learned to obey, but it is no good without the right motive.

Obedience must be quick and out of love and trust. I take no pleasure in obedience done out of habit. I don't want to be another thing you check off your list.

Come to Me with reverence, with humility, and with a right heart.

My throne room is always open and I never sleep.

Day 8

{Mark 13:17}

The end times are upon the earth even now. Pestilence, wars, famines, and rumors of wars are here now. There is no way to tell the seasons by the weather. People are acting the same as in the days of Noah.

There is no fear of Me ... no reverence. Warnings of the coming disasters are being ignored ... but the wrath in the cups will be poured out ... the horsemen will ride to the four corners of the earth.

I will come in the clouds and later I will stand on the Mount of Olives. This earth will pass away ... a new earth will be born.

With all the knowledge accessible today ... many will miss the very information they need to save their souls from hell. They will go to hell greatly educated in the things of this world thinking that their intellect is greater than their need for salvation. What does it profit man if he gains the world and loses his soul?

Eternity is a long, long time ... bitterness, unforgiveness (even of yourself) rejection of the blood sacrifice of Jesus ... aught (grievance) against each other will keep you out of the heavenly home meant for you.

Now is the time to forgive, now is the time to love your enemies, and now is the time to receive salvation ... right now.

I am loving and merciful, but I will not strive with man forever and My wrath is sure.

I would that none would perish ... but I know that many will choose it. The lust of the eyes, the lust of the flesh, and the pride of life will keep many from choosing Me.

Day 9

{James 3:11}

𝒯resh water and old should not be coming from the same source. Just so, My people must choose whom they will serve. (Me on Sunday ... the devil the rest of the week.) A good witness has one master.

The tongue is amazing in that it has not only the power of life and death, but also the power to heal and act right. Ah, but it is very hard to tame.

My followers have yet to tame it. It is full of wickedness and deceit. My people need to learn how important it is to speak forth the right thing with the right attitude.

I ask more of you as you are going through (trials) so you can see where you're really at, spiritually. Many thought they were holy until tested in the trials of adversity ... then they are able to see their real selves. Your real self is revealed by what you do and say while under pressure.

My people will do My will for time is short and I will soon come back to claim My own. Those found without spot or blemish will go home with Me. Those who are not yet ready will cry out for mercy and receive it.

Some will never believe or receive. These are destined to hell. They will teach their wicked precepts from hell. They will cry out for mercy and it will be too late.

I will have you to warn some, to get their attention. The light will shine before them, but it's up to them to follow the light.

Those who choose to follow, choose life everlasting. Those who choose not to follow, choose eternity in hell.

I will tug at the hearts of men, but I will not choose for them.

Day 10

{Galatians 6:2}

Complacency among My people is making them lazy. As long as things go well in their lives ... as long as nothing is happening to them or their family ... they are content to sit and wait for eternity in heaven.

But the church is meant to care for its members ... meant to hurt with those who are hurting, meant to be moved to the point of prayer, fasting, travail, for those who have needs.

Saved to serve and not to sit.

When Jesus walked the earth, He knew He would be going back to heaven. He could have easily sat back and waited, but He, as the church today, recognized the urgency of helping those in need ... physically, spiritually, emotionally ... even financially (coin in fish's mouth).

You have power from on high to demonstrate the awesome work of Almighty God right now, right here. This is not so people can look at other people and lift them up ... but so the God of all creation can be recognized and glorified.

He is worthy of ALL praise at ALL times.

Bernadette Hanson

The angels are perplexed at times at the way God is treated so lightly ... how He is taken for granted. He does not even owe us our next breath and no one is guaranteed tomorrow.

Saints are going home early because had they stayed, they would have strayed away ... that is mercy. Did I not say that I would that you be either cold or hot, but if you are luke warm; I will spit you from My mouth?

Love Me as I love you, with a passionate love, a love that grows ever stronger, a love that does not wax and wane.

Day 11

{John 14:12}

My power will be manifested in the earth in these end times as never before. It will be seen in the weather (tornados, earthquakes, hurricanes, etc.) and in healings as never before (limbs and organs will be restored, blind eyes will open, the deaf will hear, cancers will disappear).

This is the time of "greater works" (spoken of in the book of John). Many will come to know Me and receive Me ... a great revival. There will also be great prejudice and harassment for My own.

This is the beginning of persecutions for Christians, and it will only get worse. My people will have to walk very closely to Me; they will have to know My Word for themselves ... for they will be challenged every day. They must walk blameless and they must walk in love.

The enemy will attack on every side ... at the same time I will give new (spiritual) weapons ... love and humility, an attitude of serving ... a soft word breaketh the bone and turns away wrath.

The enemy will say, "Look what is going on ... how can your God allow this ... does He even care ... where is He now?"

Yet, I will be as close to My own as their next breath ... they will be protected and provided for ... they will not be harmed by the calamities that surround them ... as in Goshen when the Israelites and their families were spared in the midst of all the things (plagues) rained down on the Egyptians.

Persecution for My sake will be everywhere and is here, even now. This is a prelude to My return ... a time of great sorrow and a time of great expectation. I will give My own joy in spite of their circumstances.

Day 12

{Matthew 24:24}

I will speak again of things to come. There is a revival of the church coming that the world has never seen before. Many, many will be saved, healed and delivered. At the same time many will have their faith wax cold.

Counterfeit miracles will abound ... that is why you must study My Word ... to know the real true miracles from the counterfeit ones ... especially the healings that will occur ... Mine will be healed completely and permanently ... the counterfeit will heal and the sickness will recur.

People of high intelligence will attribute some of My healings to luck, circumstance, happenstance, spontaneous remission of disease ... or to something man has done (medical treatment). Woe unto him who takes My glory ... they will experience the same disease they have claimed to heal.

A one world global community is being formed even now ... one world government, one world economy, and one world religion. Woe unto them that accept this. My Word warns of these things. Even now, there are ID chips being developed for insertion in a person's hand that will contain general, medical, and financial information.

But I will always make a way for My remnant to have what they need without succumbing to the plan of the evil one. No matter what it looks like ... I AM in control ... I know My own and their protection and provision is sure.

My own will not lack ... and if they can receive it ... they will be prosperous. Piety does not go hand in hand with lack.

My holy ones will walk in the abundance meant for them.

Day 13

{Psalms 42:5}

*L*et us speak of hope ... hope gives strength to the weary ... strength to carry on in diverse trials. A person without hope is like a dry and brittle bone ... easily broken and completely depleted.

The enemy will try desperately to take away hope. Faith and hope work hand in hand ... faith believes the unseen ... hope gives strength to stand until faith is made visible. The world sorely needs hope right now.

If there is no hope, there is no reason to reconcile and work together. A people without hope will surely die ... they will give up ... dry up ... waste away. It is better to be angry than to lose hope ... there is passion and life in anger. Faith in Jesus Christ and hope in life eternal is strength for living.

Joy also works with hope ... even if there is only a little hope ... joy can be found. Joy goes beyond strength ... it's a bubbling force that renews the spirit. Joy to the spirit is like food to the body.

Hope, joy, and faith will bring many through the trying times yet to come. They give supernatural strength and restoration to the spirit. The spirit man must be healthy for the physical body to be healthy.

Many of My own though affected by physical ailments are yet kept because of their spirit which is healthy.

All that you require is found in My presence. The cares of this world fade when you're in My presence. Those who make a habit of spending time with Me will walk in health and strength and My power will be manifested in their lives.

Day 14

{I Peter 5:7}

*P*eace soothes the spirit and mind and allows the physical body to relax enough to receive healing. Whenever you pray for a physical healing for someone, pray also for peace of mind.

Peace is a rare and precious commodity now. If you do not have peace ... you will not have physical rest (trouble sleeping) and your body will become weak and susceptible to all kinds of sickness and disease. But I will keep those in perfect peace whose mind is stayed on Me.

Fear works to take peace away ... worry and doubt work to take peace away. If you give in to these because of what you see, what you hear, what you feel ... your body is in jeopardy of becoming sick ... are not the hospitals full of people whose disease started in the mind (worry, doubt, fear) and became physical manifestations ... gastric problems, heart problems, cancer. Yes, cancer can start from fear ... fear of lack of finances, fear of what will happen on the job or to your children.

Fear, worry and doubt trigger stress ... this depletes the natural mechanism placed in your body to heal and repair itself, the immune system. Your body is meant to self repair, not receive drug after drug which in itself creates other/new problems.

Have I not said, "Cast your cares upon Me?" Have I not told you how to keep your mind free from fear, worry, and doubt ... take every thought captive ... keep your mind stayed on Me ... guard your mind ... think on things that are lovely, noble, good (Philippians 4).

Your mind is very powerful and has the creative power to heal or allow disease ... choose life ... choose Me.

I would that you prosper AND BE IN HEALTH even as your soul prospers.

Day 15

{I Timothy 6:6}

Contentment with godliness is great gain. To be content in whatever your circumstances are is to have peace of mind. You cannot have lack when you are content, because whether you have a little or a lot, it is enough ... therefore there is no lack.

To covet is the opposite of being content with who you are and what you have. This comes from comparing yourself to someone else. I have made you ... each of you ... unique and special ... you all have anointings and ministries ... yet you reject that which you have and covet that which you have not. What a waste of time!

To covet is to be ungrateful with what you have been given. To covet what someone else has will only bring anxiety, frustration, and jealousy. Each one's gifts are meant to work together ... to be given to each other to build the Kingdom of God.

How can you be a Preacher when you have a Prophet's anointing? How can you be a Psalmist with a Teacher's anointing? Let each one go forth in their own gifts. Seek to please ME. Too many want the praise of men ... NOT SO.

Even if no one understands your ministry, go forth in it because it pleases ME. *It is better to obey God than man.*

Remember that man's favor is fickle ... you will gain it one day and lose it the next.

Please ME ... I do not change. Jealousy is a divider among men, and I want My own to be united. Jealousy leads to anger which leads to rage which leads to murder.

Be content where you are, who you are, and with your anointing. To be ungrateful is to be out of My will.

Every ministry is important in My eyes. Trust Me in My choice for you.

Day 16

{Romans 4:17}

*S*trength is found as you speak forth My Word. It has power to change things. When the Word is spoken, things begin to happen in the spiritual realm. Soon after, things change in the physical realm.

Prayer can be likened to a seed ... this seed is watered (fed) by faith. Once it starts to grow, results will be seen in the physical. Prayer touches My very heart. Prayer takes humility ... the act of admitting that only I can change things.

There are many powerful life changing prayers in My Word. Make no mistake ... they are NOT a magic formula to produce a desired effect ... but words with power that are intended to be spoken with reverence and humility.

Faith takes submission ... the act of waiting on Me for whatever you need for whatever length of time it takes to manifest in the physical. I look on your heart ... your attitude MUST be right when speaking to Me.

A humble and submitted heart moves Me. The effectual fervent prayer of the righteous man truly does avail much ... miracles have happened because of faith and submission.

Anger and an attitude of entitlement will create a distance between us. You know not the plans set forth for you ... the road you will travel on this earth is not guaranteed to be trouble free. To the contrary, adversity must come to shape you into the one that I intended you to be before you were even born.

Be assured that each one's life is carefully planned before their first breath is drawn. Stubbornness and rebellion will halt My plan for you ... but repentance will bring you back to right standing.

Day 17

{Isaiah 58:6}

*L*et us speak of prayer and fasting. Fasting is the way to bring the physical body under subjection ... to purify the thoughts ... to become humble. Those who make a regular habit of fasting will hear Me clearly.

There are times when I will call a fast for a specific reason in a church ... this unites the church and makes way for My presence and My power to manifest in a supernatural way.

Fasting, when done in obedience to Me, will break the yokes and bring deliverance to those who fast for the right reason and with the right attitude. Just as with giving ... with praise ... with obedience ... fasting must be done the way I intended ... with the right attitude of the heart.

Fasting and prayer are powerful together ... this is the way to break down strongholds to bring deliverance from demonic attacks. Fasting will bring you into My presence and where I am ... demons must flee.

Darkness and light cannot occupy the same space. Fasting is a purifier ... for the spirit ... for the body ... for the mind. Fasting is not something done only by the early church, but is meant for My people right now.

Things will be activated in the spirit realm as the flesh submits and stands humbly before Me. Jesus fasted often and I sustained Him with "food" for His spirit man that His Apostles knew not.

Fasting during trials strengthens the spirit man (Jesus in the desert). The body is meant to be purified during seasons of fasting. Fasting as a church is a unifying force and when My people stand united according to My Word, I will withhold no good thing from them, but move quickly on their behalf.

Day 18

{Romans 14:23}

Complaining, grumbling, and murmuring will all take you away from your blessings and delay your blessings ... they are the opposite of trust and faith. Without faith ... apart from believing what I say is true ... you cannot please Me.

I only ask that when you pray ... when you are given a prophetic word ... believe it and receive it right away. My timing is not your timing and you may have to wait for a while ... even years ... for it to manifest in the physical ... but My Word is sure.

I cannot lie ... My Word will not come back void, but will accomplish that which I sent it to do. No matter what things look like My Word is sure.

Imagine what the Israelites thought as the Egyptians pursued them into the Red Sea ... but they saw victory over their enemies that day and were never again pursued or persecuted by that enemy.

Instead of complaining, which delays your blessing, thank Me and confess and agree with My Word that your blessing will happen. When you and I are in agreement ... the blessings will flow ... this is when I open up the windows of heaven and pour out.

Bernadette Hanson

Thank me in all things at all times ... this is My will for you. Did I not say rejoice always? Your attitude must be one of joyful expectation (like a child opening a gift).

My Word is sure ... My will is to bless and prosper you ... but you must have the right attitude in your heart.

You must remember, hold on to, and confess the prophesies said over you ... they will and must come to pass.

My plans for you are good and not evil, but many times you will need to wait upon them. Believe Me, things are being arranged and orchestrated in ways you cannot see from the moment My promise is given.

Day 19

{Psalms 37:4}

Blessings are about to flow in the earth as never before. There will be miracles and healings that the world has not seen. Yes ... there will be terrible things ... wars, famines, pestilence, cruelty ... but there will also be supernatural moves and provisions and interventions.

My people will be delivered from the attacks of their enemies. The more they attack ... the more I will bless My people ... My faithful ones. Faith in times of trial (the sacrifice of faith) deeply moves Me, and will not go unrewarded.

You will be rewarded in this time, in this earth. Many of My own do not think that blessings and rewards are for their time on earth ... of course they are!

When you delight yourself in Me I will give you the desires of your heart. When you put Me first, blessings will flow. When you desire Me ... love Me ... obey Me first, I will pour out blessings.

I am full, so when you minister to Me, I automatically overflow ... blessings will follow each one that delights themselves in Me.

Every good and great gift is from above ... they were created to bless My people during their time on earth. The earth was originally created to be a place of great beauty, great peace ... a place that reflected My glory and inspired My praise.

Even today I paint the skies and blow gentle winds ... did you see or stop to appreciate what I painted for you today?

I whisper words of beauty and kindness and love ... did you hear them today?

Ministering angels walk the earth to serve Me ... to protect My own ... were you blessed by one of them today?

Like the wind ... even though you cannot see Me ... I constantly surround you and the evidence of My presence is ever with you.

Day 20

{Matthew 7:15}

The devil and his fallen angels roam the world seeking whom they may deceive and devour. They entice, they tempt, they lie, they cheat, they steal ... they have a murderous spirit.

Know this ... they cannot do anything without permission. Why do you think they pose as angels of light and wolves in sheep's clothing? They are masters at deception.

They mix outright lies with the truth in My Word. Again I say ... they can do nothing without permission ... they must gain access to a willing individual and consent is assumed when a person partakes of their offerings ... occult practices and games , tarot and card readings, palm and tea readings, horoscope readings ... willing worship to any other god but Me ... revenge, gossiping, backbiting, coveting, jealousy, anger, rage.

When you partake, you open the door to: oppression, depression, possession, sickness, bondage, and all evil things.

Learn to stay in My presence and to declare My Word to the hurting souls (deliverance). Keep your thoughts and your words pure ... walk in forgiveness ... repent quickly ... walk in love.

Your spirit man wants to follow Me, but the flesh is truly weak. Strengthen your physical body through prayer and fasting ... partake (regularly) of the Lord's Supper. My body was given to bring you health, salvation and deliverance.

Know ye not that ye are the temple of the Holy Spirit purchased at a great price?

Temples should be clean ... holy ... pure ... a place prepared and kept for the Holy Spirit to dwell in.

Don't grieve Me by taking the blood sacrifice of the spotless lamb, Jesus Christ, lightly.

Day 21

{Zechariah 13:9}

Child, let your tears flow ... don't ever be ashamed to cry out to Me. I am as close as your next breath, your next heartbeat, and I want you to cast all your cares upon Me.

No matter how it feels, I am working this out for your good and no, I will not give you more than you can bear.

Remember the goldsmith how, when he is refining the gold to remove impurities he cannot ... even for a second ... take his eyes off the gold ... to stop too soon is to leave impurities and to stop too late is to let the gold break down. The timing must be perfect ... must be done by a master goldsmith.

I will not let you go through to the point of breaking your spirit ... neither will I let up until the refining removes that which is impure. Trials show you weak spots ... things that need to be changed and let go of in your life.

Do not despise the refining for this is how you are molded into the one that I intend you to be. And yes, during the trying times of refining, I will require you to minister to others, to show My love in the midst of your own hard times. This is the breaking ... where you are decreased and I am increased ... some give up too soon and have to go through the refining process over and over.

Cry out to Me, trust Me, pray to Me, but do not give up when in the refining fire for pure gold is about to manifest ... strength and joy and blessings are waiting to overtake you.

I am with you, I am for you, I will not leave you for you are My very own purchased with a precious price.

Salvation is free, but to walk in your anointing and appointed ministry many trials will be endured for refining and purifying must be done.

Day 22

{Psalms 34:19}

Trusting Me is something you must learn ... this is done through trials. When I deliver you from your afflictions, you learn to trust Me. The problem is that after the deliverance, My people soon forget what I have done for them.

To develop humility, trials will happen over and over. Humility ... understanding that you can do nothing apart from Me ... this is pleasing to Me. I hate a haughty spirit and an attitude of (self) pride.

Humility leads to trust which leads to faith. Faith ... waiting and believing (on Me) ... pleases Me. Pride comes before the fall and humility before honor. This is why some of My people have not yet been elevated ... their spirits have not developed humility.

To elevate someone with a haughty spirit is to set them up for a fall. You cannot go forth in your anointing or your ministry in the way I intended without humility.

Jesus was a humble and meek servant. Remember that meekness does not in any way mean weakness. For meekness is strength under control ... the ability to keep silent when being attacked by the enemy ... the ability to forgive, loose and release in the midst of fiery trials.

In order to go to the next (higher) level you must learn obedience by staying humble through adversity. It's tempting to give in to anger and self pity, but these will only allow you to repeat the same lessons over and over.

I see every tear, I hear every thought, and I see the attitude of men's hearts behind the false humility that they display. Anger and rage are not only damaging to the spirit and soul, but to the physical body.

You cannot be My ambassadors and display godly attitudes while harboring anger. Loose and release your frustrations to Me quickly and I will give you peace.

Day 23

{Philippians 4:11}

Contentment with godliness is great gain ... do you know why? Contentment is a choice you make to accept who you are, what you have and whatever circumstances you find yourself in ... to choose to be satisfied.

How many times have I told you not to compare yourself with others? Each is given their own path ... their own trials ... their own blessings. Your life was planned out just for you. To not be content with what I have given you is to be ungrateful.

To envy or covet what someone else has can only lead to frustration, anxiety, anger and jealousy. Lack of self control has many of My own in financial debt and overweight physically. They are tired and worn out chasing things that I would gladly give them if they only waited on Me to do so.

I see the desires of your heart ... and I will gladly give it to you IF you delight in Me ... if you put Me first ... if you desire Me more than the things of this earth ... don't you realize that they are only temporary?

The most beautiful objects on this earth will eventually rot away. The yearning and emptiness you try to fill was meant for a Holy treasure ... a relationship with Me. That will fulfill and satisfy and complete you. The void you feel cannot be satisfied with food, sex, clothes, cars or any temporary thing on this earth.

Delight yourself in Me. Don't you know that I long to have an intimate relationship with all My children? My love is not comparable to the love between a man and a woman or the love of brothers and sisters ... My love is deep ... My love is wide ... My love sent Jesus to the cross.

Put Me first and you will be well satisfied and I will give you the desires of your heart.

Day 24

{Romans 8:31}

My daughter, like Martha, you are troubled by many things. First, know this, that I am for you and if I am for you ... who can be against you? I hold the hearts of men in My hands and I turn them whither so ever way I will. Nothing shall by any means hurt you and yes, this battle belongs to Me.

Leave room for the wrath of God ... vengeance is Mine ... I will repay. I require that you confess your sin, that you bless those that curse you, and pray for those that despitefully use you.

Loose and release your troubles to Me for I am well able to fix what is wrong. Do not worry, do not fret, be anxious for nothing for I am with you always ... you are My very own ... I will not leave or forsake you.

Praise Me now because there is a wonderful blessing waiting for all who put their trust in Me. This too shall pass ... have I not said it? Trust Me, dear one, I hold you in the palm of My hand.

Times of trials and tribulations must come, but they will not last. This is the time to submit and surrender ... your enemies cannot do anything unless I allow it. Lift up your countenance for My joy is your strength.

Bernadette Hanson

To see you acting victorious, to hear you praise Me, to know your faith is in Me, this gives Me joy which in turn, gives you strength.

The enemy is busy and more cruel and devious than ever. At the same time, My power in the earth is greater than ever.

Do not ever doubt that I am in control ... that the earth and the fullness thereof belong to Me. I am for you, trust Me.

This too shall pass.

Day 25

{2 Chronicles 20:15}

*D*id I not tell you that the best is yet to come? When you release your faith ... I release My blessings. Blessings and miracles are yet to come. Trust Me always.

If you will only stop and listen, I will speak to you ... doesn't My Word say, "To those who have a (spiritual) ear, let them hear." I have made My Word simple enough for a child to understand ... don't make it complicated ... I want you to read and understand.

My yoke is easy and My burden is light. I am here to fight your battles ... when you cry, I'm there. When you praise, when you become still and listen for My voice, when you decide to step out in faith and trust Me ... I'm there.

I will not leave my own even as a shepherd will not leave his sheep. I will correct you and direct you, and I will chasten those whom I love ... but I will not leave you. Only come to me with a willing and clean attitude of the heart. I cannot resist a humble and reverent heart.

No good thing will I withhold from those who truly love Me. Miracles and supernatural blessings are being poured out even now. All will know that I alone am God ... there is none like unto Me.

I rule the waters, I blow the winds, I give and I take away. All souls will bow down before Me and receive their due recompense and reward.

Only mercy keeps the judgment until its due time. I would that each one receives Me, but I know that some will not.

I have wept for those who have chosen hell over Me. Yet, free will allows each one to choose their place in eternity.

Day 26

{Psalms 46:10}

Be still and know that I am God ... I alone ... there is none like unto Me. I am not some uncaring and distant ruler that is uninterested in My people. I cry when you cry, I laugh when you laugh, I hurt when you hurt.

I walked the earth in a flesh body ... I was tempted in all the ways that you are. I have compassion and great love for each one I have created. You are made in My image.... I have created each one to reflect My attributes.

Each one has been given distinct gifts and skills. Each one has a specific ministry. I was not always understood or welcomed when I walked the earth ... neither will you be. Purpose in your heart to please Me, and I will make a way for you with man.

Do what I ask regardless of how man may react ... please Me and I will give you favor. Even your enemies will bless you and walk in peace with you ... they won't understand why they're doing it ... but they will do it nonetheless.

I want to fellowship, I want to reveal the deep things if only you will spend time with Me and listen.

Bernadette Hanson

This is a time of great knowledge ... much information ... the things that are most needful can be understood as you spend quiet time with Me.

Yes, I want to hear your prayers, but are you willing to wait long enough to hear My answers to them? I know what you will ask for before you say it ... I asked you to let your requests be made known so we can fellowship ... so there is communication not just from you to Me, but from Me to you.

Day 27

{Isaiah 26:3}

Let us speak of health and peace. I will keep you in perfect peace whose mind is stayed on Me. There are so many pressures in the world today ... so much stress. It creates an atmosphere of great mental turmoil.

People cannot sleep because their minds are racing ... there is great unrest. If you cannot have peaceful rest, your physical body will suffer. You are meant and designed to heal and restore energy with physical rest.

I would that you seek Me when you cannot sleep ... put away the pills; the alcohol ... let Me give you true rest. There are always counterfeit ways to receive what you need, but My ways are better.

I will give My beloved sweet sleep. I will bless in great ways and add no sorrow to it. All that you need ... I have it ... just ask. You have not because you ask not. I want you to come to Me with all requests ... I want you to come to Me with all decisions.

You can rest in Me. You can trust Me ... even if I say No ... it is to bring about good in your life. I see from beginning to end ... I know the perfect timing to allow things to happen in your life.

You can go against My will, but your ways are not My ways and you will soon be praying to be delivered from what you have brought upon yourself.

Trust Me when I say that I love you, that I know the plans I have for you. Turn to Me often during the day … pray without ceasing.

Every day is planned, every day is filled with blessings … it's up to you to receive them or go your own way and miss them. I would that you follow My plan and be blessed.

Day 28

{Revelation 12:10}

The devil and his angels want to constantly remind you of past sins and mistakes. Believe me when I tell you ... if you repent from your heart and ask for forgiveness ... it's done.

It's removed from you as far as the east is from the west. Forgiven sins are thrown into the sea of forgetfulness. When your mind is attacked ... speak forth My Word. Use the sword of the Spirit to fight back ... the devil himself cannot refute My Word and My word will not come back void ... every time it is spoken things are set in motion in the spirit realm ... battles are fought ... strongholds are broken.

The enemy wants to shut your mouth ... wants you to feel as though you are not worthy to speak My Word ... you don't have to be worthy, you just have to be under the blood (of Jesus).

Use the shield of faith to protect your mind ... faith believes Me only and not the lies and attacks from the enemy. When you speak forth the Word you increase your faith. Faith comes by hearing and hearing by the Word of God.

Want more faith? Speak more of My Word.

You will fall sometimes, make mistakes, you will miss the mark (sin) ... that is why there was a perfect blood sacrifice ... that is why you have an advocate (mediator) ... that is why you have repentance ... to get back into right standing with Me.

I know the flesh is weak, but let the weak say they are strong ... I am your strength.

You have a high priest who prays for you at all times. Do not believe the enemy ... take his power away by believing Me.

Day 29

{Joshua 24:15}

*D*emonic attacks will not stop or prevent the miracles and blessings that are for this time ... they will only bring My own closer to Me. They will serve to push My people closer than ever before. They will seek refuge in Me, and I will deliver them from all evil.

Evil times are upon the earth. Things that would not have been tolerated even ten years ago are now common place. Anti-Christian attacks are common place. Israel is more of a target than ever before as are the countries that help her.

My beloved Israel will always have a remnant ... will always have Divine protection and provision. As it goes in the Middle East ... so goes the world.

Now is the time to focus on salvation ... the things of this world will pass away ... much quicker than you can imagine. People need salvation right now ... pray for it ... proclaim the Good News.

Be about the business of building the Kingdom ... all such things that you need will be provided. I weep for each soul that does not receive salvation. Each one MUST hear so they can make a choice.

Bernadette Hanson

My people need to move now ... the purpose of the church is to reach the lost. Many lives hang in the balance ... many are in the valley of decision ... the Gospel MUST reach all four corners of the world.

I have sent My own even to the remotest parts of the earth. All will know that I alone am God ... that eternity is real ... that hell is real ... that each one MUST make a choice to receive or discard the blood sacrifice of the Spotless Lamb.

His sacrifice was beyond price and each one must know it.

Day 30

{Revelation 3:12}

The day is coming soon when I will again set foot on this earth (for the last time). For this earth will pass away and there will be a new one and a New Jerusalem ... that will be a time of great joy.

Even now the earth groans as the time of its passing draws near. The last days are a time of great tribulation ... unprecedented changes in climate ... great and terrible forces of nature ... storms, winds, hurricanes, earthquakes, floods, famines, pestilence (diseases).

Yet, did I not say on the cross, "It Is Finished."? The future has been written in My Word. The steps have been orchestrated and circumstances have been set in motion.

Truly, time is short ... the most urgent need is for salvation.

The Gospel is already on its journey around the world ... oh, that the world would listen. The things of the devil ... these, people believe ... there is fear of evil.

What you should fear is the One who can destroy your body and soul!

Bernadette Hanson

Where is the reverent fear of God? I will not strive with man forever. The time has been set and salvation is offered as a gift right now. To every thing is appointed a time and a season and the time for salvation is now.

Put away pride, put away anger, put away prejudice ... speak My Word. Let people know that I'm alive and well and tell them the Good News of the Gospel.

I need living Epistles. How can one choose if they have not been given the choices?

Speak My Word.

30 Days with JESUS

Notes:

Revelation of the Front Cover

I would like you to take a closer look at the cover on this book and think about something. Do you see how small the people are and how big the majesty of God's creation is? This is the perspective that the Lord is asking us to have...to see how huge, how incredible big He is in comparison to our problems. Do you know how to meditate on the Lord ... if you know how to worry, then you know how to meditate. Worrying is going over and over the problem. Meditating on the Lord is going over and over the solution. We can choose to concentrate on the small temporary "light afflictions" of our lives, or we can choose to trust Him.

Joshua 24:15 *"And if it seem evil unto you to serve the LORD, choose you this day whom ye will serve; whether the gods which your fathers served that [were] on the other side of the flood, or the gods of the Amorites, in whose land ye dwell: but as for me and my house, we will serve the LORD."*

Many blessings,

    b

30 MORE DAYS WITH JESUS

Day 31

{Matthew 11:28}

Come unto Me all you that are heavy burdened and I will give you rest. Why are you so worried and anxious? I will keep those in perfect peace whose mind is stayed on Me. Your body is not meant to take on excessive consistent stress.

Cast your cares unto Me for I truly do care for you. Sickness and disease come when you are overstressed, fearful, anxious, fatigued or depressed. Have you not seen that My Word says be anxious for nothing, that the joy of the Lord is your strength?

Give Me your troubles, your fears, your doubts ... release them to Me and have faith that I am always working them out for your good. Walk in faith, walk in joy and you will walk in strength.

Stay close to Me and receive the comfort you need from My Word. I will comfort you so you may comfort others who are going through the same situation.

When you release your hurts to Me and receive My love and comfort, then you can show My love to others by giving them the same.

Day 32

{Isaiah 5:20}

Cling to Me, cleave to Me, and stay very close for times are perilous, men are desperate and the enemy knows his time is short. Desperate and violent acts of the enemy abound ... where there is no trust, there is no hope ... when good is called evil and evil is called good and evil acts hide behind the mask of "tolerance" ... there are things that are not meant to be tolerated.

All things work for the good, but all things are not meant to bring good into your life. Some things will bring hurt, pain or disappointment ... these are to strengthen you, to build your character, to show you how much you need Me ... to cause you to run to Me and stay close.

As long as you are on this earth, there will be trials and tribulations ... they will work patience and absolute confirmation that apart from Me you can do nothing.

All will come to Me either by choice or by circumstance. Each one will stand before Me for an accounting. I will in no wise cast anyone out who comes to Me with a broken and contrite spirit, and I will forgive and receive them.

Day 33

{I John 1:9}

There are those who think that there is no hope of restoration in relationship to Me because of what they have done. This is a lie and completely untrue.

You can always come back into right standing with Me by repenting with your heart of your sin. What have you done, what have you thought, what have you imagined or have had an attitude about, what have you said that is not covered by My blood sacrifice?

When you repent from your heart, ALL is forgiven, all filthiness is cleansed and all is cast into the sea of forgetfulness where your sins are as far from you as the east is from the west.

I am waiting to forgive you ... your sins are already paid for ... why do you not receive the forgiveness that is already yours?

This is a time of great restoration ... it will not always be so ... for I will not strive with man always. If you insist on believing a lie ... I will send a strong delusion so you may do so.

My hearts desire is to restore the fellowship between you and Me ... come unto Me ... repent ... let us sup together.

Day 34

{I Samuel 15:22}

Truly I have blessed you, and the blessings will continue. I have always blessed the obedience of My children. Hearken unto My voice for in it are many blessings.

My children, Israel, have been disciplined for not listening to Me. Listening is better than the fat of rams and obedience is better than a sacrifice.

In these last days I will begin to pour out My Spirit and those who hearken will be mightily blessed. I long to be heard, I long to bless My children for their obedience.

Many come to talk to Me, but few come to listen and it's in listening that you learn what I want you to do in this earth. The noises of the world are distracting ... the cares of this world are meant to turn you to Me.

In this age where there are so many distractions, truly having a quiet time with Me ... just to listen ... will bring much peace.

Peace is a precious commodity now. In listening, you will learn and gain peace. My will is that My people listen and serve.

Day 35

{Isaiah 55:8}

*Y*esterday I talked about listening; today I will talk about obedience. Obedience is better than a sacrifice because it comes from the heart. Truly, someone obeys out of love ... it is indeed sometimes a sacrifice to do so and to Me this is beautiful.

Those who obey despite how they feel in their present circumstances will truly reap a wonderful blessing.

I blessed Abraham, David, Moses and Paul because of their obedience, and I am still looking for those who will obey Me today. If only you will trust Me enough to obey quickly and without question ... but no one listens long enough or frequently enough to recognize My voice.... And, even if it is clearly Me speaking, there are many who question or second guess Me.

My ways are not your ways ... My instructions and requests will at times sound very strange ... but trust Me because My plan is much better than any plan you can think of.

Going forward with your plan is a sure way to end up frustrated, angry and confused. Listen to My voice ... and obey.

Bernadette Hanson

Day 36

{3 John 1:2}

Healing is the children's bread ... something they must have ... especially now. Demonic attack is at an all time high and yet, if you can receive it, My miracles (especially healing) are here for the asking and overflowing.

My children should be ... need to be ... well enough to minister to the unsaved at this time ... a time when the world needs to see My power ... a time when the world needs to see I'm real ... now more than ever.

The lame will walk, the deaf will hear, the blind will see, the dead will rise ... cancer will completely disappear ... all by MY power ... because it is My will for it to happen.

This is the time for greater works ... greater attacks ... greater faith.

Truly man has become more proud than ever and when My people are told that their condition is untreatable, they give up. But this is the time when My power is stronger and more available.

I have the last word on healing ... not man. I will heal anyone who dares to believe Me and cries out for My help.

Day 37

{I Peter 2:24}

More about healing ... some ask for it, but really do not receive because they enjoy the sympathy from others more than the actual healing. Many times unbelievers genuinely desire My healing gift and receive it because at the time, they are ready. I will at times impart My healing anointing to unbelievers to create a longing and desire in the hearts of My own people to seek Me for the same.... My very own who do not believe or receive the very gift intended for them. *God uses jealousy to stir His people to turn back to Him when they have gone astray* ... (Romans 10:19 and 11:11)

My Word describes how I endured 39 stripes ... to cover healing under every type of sickness and disease. Truly, if you can receive it, your disease must go because the price has already been paid ... in MY blood.

Stubbornness, pride, unbelief ... all these stop the very gift meant for My people. Healing is a sign to the unbeliever to let them know that My very own are set apart ... special and beloved unto Me.

But I will heal all who cry out with a faith filled heart. Faith is the key that unlocks many doors ... doors to the treasures I have stored up for those who truly love Me.

Bernadette Hanson

Yes, you can have heavenly treasures on earth when you believe enough to use the key of faith ... you must be humble enough to receive My gifts ... you must admit that you need Me and cannot do these things on your own.

Believe Me and doors will open.

Day 38

{Acts 3:19}

Quiet times are times of refreshing. I have put in you a need for these times ... not only to come into My presence, but to be refreshed ... spirit, soul and body. Every part of you needs rest and refreshment.

A tired spirit or soul leads to depression, anger, frustration ... this is not My will for you. My will is peace and joy in spite of circumstances. If your spirit-man is refreshed, you can handle anything in the natural.

Constant grumbling and complaining deplete the energy in the (human) spirit ... you need this energy to discern the things of the (Holy) Spirit to accomplish what is impossible in the natural ... to refresh and renew your faith.

Do you know that faith really does move mountains ... come into My presence and be refreshed and watch the mountains in your life move ... mountains of debt and fear ... of worry.

My will is for My children not only to be joyful but to be powerful ... fully charged spiritually to do the work that only the (Holy) Spirit can do. To be the witness and ambassador I require and desire.

Bernadette Hanson

So few are willing to come and be refreshed in the spirit ... they would rather beg and complain. But My will is that My people have power and dominion over this earth to do the greater works I speak of in Acts.

Day 39

{I Corinthians 10:13}

*D*ifficult days come not only so you'll appreciate the good days, but to keep you humble and close to me.

I will never give you more than you can bear ... even though it may feel that way. I see your spirit man ... and your spirit is much stronger than your physical body. Your spirit man may also be attacked and wounded but each time you let Me do My work in you ... your spirit man will become stronger and stronger ... this is what I mean when I say be ye perfect or mature.

Mature Christians can take more and bounce back quicker from attacks. It does not please Me to see My children wounded, but when this brings them closer to Me, this is definitely My plan.

My plan is for your good no matter what it looks like ... dross (sin), stubbornness, pride ... these must be removed in order for you to be used ... to fulfill your part in My plan.

Yes, everyone has a portion in My plan. What I want is a people without spot or blemish ... one who is humble, yet strong; one that obeys through the trials.

Many blessings are coming for those who obey through adversity ... for this is truly a sweet fragrance unto Me.

Bernadette Hanson

Love me, put Me first, obey ... so simple ... and yet I know it is difficult.

Ask for My strength, I'm never tired. I will replenish and refill the strength to every weary soul.

Day 40

{John 3:16}

I would that My people stand united ... one voice ... one purpose ... one plan. The days appointed to reach the lost are right now. So many are crying out to Me ... asking Me to manifest Myself in their lives ... in the schools ... in the jails ... in the hospitals.

Weary broken souls waiting to hear the "good news". They know there is a better way ... something more that can't be seen with physical eyes or heard with the natural ear.

They cry out because instinctively they know I am the way.

The world system has failed them ... families have given up on them. In desperation they cry out. My church will minister to the broken hearted, to the outcasts and those forsaken by the world. I don't give up on anyone ... even when they give up on Me.

The blood sacrifice on the cross is for "whosoever" will. I would that every precious soul be saved. I will give wisdom to each one that asks for it ... you will need it more than ever now. Let Me give you the words to minister with ... I know each soul personally. Some need a soft word ... some need the facts and the truth laid out.

My laborers will reap a great end time harvest. The hardships, trials and stressors of this time have served to bring souls closer to Me. I will not always strive with man for even the time of grace has an appointed beginning and end.

The laborers will be rewarded for their work ... peace, joy, untold blessings ... the work comes first and then the recompense.

Day 41

{Hebrews 1:13-14}

*L*et us speak of angels. I describe many types of angels in My Word. Cherubim, Seraphim, holy angels that praise ... that kiss My face, warfaring angels ... ministering angels ... angels that bring messages ... angels that fight in the heavenly realms ... angels that surround and protect My own.

Angels are spirit beings sent to minister to souls on earth. They know they are not made of flesh as men are. Because they spend time in My presence, they are perplexed when men do not choose to praise Me ... to receive Me.

I send them to the four corners of the earth to comfort, to warfare, to protect, to minister. They will not accept praise ... that belongs to Me. There are angels on the earth at all times ... that is why I said, "Beware of how you entertain strangers ... it may be an angel."

They are still sent forth to bring strength and good tidings to the weary. When they warfare ... demons flee. Man has been made a little lower than the angels ... just for a set time. In the end My own will judge the angels who fell with Satan ... the very ones who torment and accuse them now.

Every angel is under My command ... what they do, I allow. Fallen angels are only allowed to come against man for a set time. Their judgment is sure. Their works will be held against them. They will answer for every deed. But even they must go forth to fulfill My plan.

They will force many to cry out to Me, to seek Me. I will deliver when My own cry out.

Day 42

{Genesis 1:26}

I have made man a little lower than the angels ... but they will only be lower for yet a little while. Man is made in Our image while angels are spiritual beings. Man and angels serve Me out of free will.

Because I love man so much, My son, Jesus, paid for their sins with His own precious blood. He redeemed their souls from sin and spiritual death ... dying as the spotless lamb ... once and for all.

This sacrifice is never to be taken lightly. Celebrating the Lord's Supper/Communion ... that time when His death and sacrifice is remembered ... is never to be taken lightly.

The sin of all mankind was upon His innocent head and His innocent blood bought back all things stolen by the enemy ... everlasting life in the presence of Almighty God, fellowship with God, physical health.

If you would only stop and realize what Jesus' blood actually did for you....

Faith in His perfect blood sacrifice is still reconciling souls back to God ... still working healing miracles, still protecting and keeping My own today.

It grieves Me when this sacrifice is taken lightly ... when Communion is taken unworthily ... do you not know the price paid on the cross?

The price was so great that it covered every sin of every man for all time.

I would that My people ponder the blood sacrifice that set them free ... every day. For every day, as the accuser of the brethren comes against My people, Jesus proclaims their punishment has been fulfilled ... paid in full.

Ponder this every day.

Day 43

{Psalms 121:4}

I would that none of My own would feel helpless. For I am the eternal hope. I know all and I see all. If only My people would ask Me for answers ... I would give them.

I don't want to see them cry ... to reach for drugs or alcohol ... there is no reason for them to do that when I can give them hope. I want them to have joy unspeakable and the peace that passes understanding.

You have not because you ask not. When you cry out to Me ... wait ... listen ... I want to give you encouraging words and understanding. Turn to Me in times of trouble. I am a very present help in times of trouble. These times must come if only to show you where your heart really is ... where you are turning to (depending on) in bad times for comfort/strength.

I never sleep or slumber ... I am here for you always. Remember that troubled times have a beginning and an end ... even though it may look like you'll never get past them ... you will.

I will not give you more than you can bear, but will make a way of escape. I know you are (but) dust ... I will not break your spirit. Times of testing will come, but they are only to prepare you, to reshape you into the one I intend you to be.

Fear not during times of testing, for I am with you always. I allow these things in your life to let you know that you can always trust Me, you can always turn to Me. I know how much you can bear.

Every time you make it past the hard times you gain strength. This life is like (the life of) grass ... short. You are being prepared for eternity.

Eternity in My presence will make all the times of hardship seem short. Hold on ... for eternity will be here sooner than you think.

Day 44

{Matthew 6:33}

Silence, reverence, awe, praise ... these will usher you into My presence. Many think they must always be loud to come into My presence ... .NOT so.

Yes, I love the joyful noise, but I also desire quiet reverence. How can you hear My still small voice when your mind is racing?

I desire to speak to each of My own every day ... to comfort them and give them words of wisdom, but I will not compete with a racing mind or a mind that clicks off rote rehearsed prayers in an attempt to check Me off their daily list of things to do.

If I manifested Myself in person, you would be too overwhelmed. You would realize that glory, reverence, praise and quiet awe, belong to Me.

As you long to commune with your children ... to hear their thoughts and spend time with them ... so I long to be with My children.

Imagine coming before My throne ... into the holiness of My presence ... this is where your troubles leave and become insignificant ... this is where miracles are born.

Bernadette Hanson

If you would only seek Me first, such things as you have need of would automatically be provided for. I want you to seek Me and praise Me (sacrifice of praise) in spite of any trials or circumstances you are going through. Seek My presence ... not My provision ... for provision will surely follow each one that earnestly seeks Me.

I will reward each one that seeks Me first (in their life). Blessings wait in abundance ... but many will miss the very blessing they need. Seek Me first ... seek Me in spite of what you're going through, for I long to pour out blessings on you.

Day 45

{Romans 12:3}

You must have faith to live in these last days. If you have no faith, you have no hope and without hope, you will perish.

I will give a measure of faith to all who ask for it, just as I did to the father of the child who was possessed (in the Bible) who said, "Help my unbelief". Those who ask humbly and sincerely shall surely receive what they need/ask for.

If you can receive what you ask for ... faith, miracles, deliverance, healing ... you will receive what you believe. Without faith, it is impossible to please Me ... so ask for it.

Ask for wisdom as well, you will need it in these last days. Wisdom will tell you what to do in confusing situations. Persecution and all sorts of demonic attacks are loosed now ... faith and wisdom will allow the peace of mind needed to quietly listen to My voice.

If you can (clearly) hear Me, I will guide you through every troubled time in your life. I am with you always, but to hear Me you will need to calmly listen ... I will not compete with worry, doubt and fear.

Believe that I have a plan for you, that I am in control, that every circumstance in your life has a purpose, that it is being worked for your good, that I will not give you more than you can bear.

Do not compare your journey with anyone else ... each one has a certain path ... a path planned just for them. My love for you is indescribable ... believe it.

Day 46

{James 4:2}

My son, My daughter, you need only ask for anything you have need of ... I will supply your needs according to My riches in glory. As My ambassadors on this earth, My children should have the best of earthly things.

This will not come without obedience. Things outside of My will for you will not be given. My own shall be servants first ... ministering to the hurting and the lost. As you go about your (heavenly) Father's business ... He will attend to your needs.

Some will not ask for what they need, thinking that this is humility ... actually it is false pride and a lack of faith in My promises. You have not because you ask not or because you ask amiss ... according to fleshly lusts and desires.

First give, first serve, first minister, first share the good news of the Gospel ... THEN ask ... for I love to give.

As soon as you realize that things that are seen are temporary ... as soon as you know their real value ... when you realize the true "worth" of things and have My (Godly) perspective ... then shall you have them.

I will not compete with the things you desire on earth ... not for your love ... not for your attention.

When you realize the value of things unseen ... then you will desire as I intended. It's hard to covet and have jealousy for the things of this earth when you realize how little value they have in eternity.

What waits for you in the heavenly realm is far above all that you could ask, think or imagine. Desire Me, desire things unseen which are eternal.

Day 47

{Genesis 6:3}

This is a time of grace ... a time when man is given many chances to come to Me, repent and be saved ... a time of mercy upon the souls of men. But I will not strive with man always ... there will come a time of judgment and no mercy. That is why this is a time of great urgency to save souls.

After this comes great revival ... in the midst of many trials. Right now salvation is free and there is only the beginning of persecution of Christians, but it's about to get worse. Salvation will come at a great price during the time of Tribulation ... now is the time for the laborer to harvest the souls.

Now is the time to believe ... now is the time to receive the truth of the Gospel ... now is the time to choose everlasting life.

Those who accept Me in faith and endure persecution for My sake will surely be blessed. Blessed is he who has not seen and yet believes. Every (set) time has an exact beginning and an exact end and My will, shall be done in the earth.

Now is the time to win souls, to witness to the lost, to minister to the brokenhearted, to deliver and set the captives free. My power will be shown in the earth and My grace and mercy are here for the asking ... but this is only for a set time.

Day 48

{Philippians 4:6}

Do you know why I said, "be anxious for nothing"? It's because the things of this world are temporary. They will all pass away ... didn't I say, "it came to pass"? My child, that the light afflictions of this world are only for a moment.

Many trials will come your way ... these are to mold you and strengthen you ... to bring you closer to Me. I know you are but dust (like grass). Even though it may feel as though you are about to break, I won't let that happen.

You are My beloved and nothing shall by any means hurt you. Trust me during trials ... My plan for you is to bring about good and not evil ... to bring (My) expected end. Know that I am as close to you as your next breath, as your next heartbeat.

Learn to cleave unto Me during hard times ... fast and pray ... loose and release your cares to Me ... I do care for you. I have already borne your burdens ... you don't have to carry them (when Jesus carried the cross). I want you to lean on Me, to depend on Me, to trust Me, to have faith no matter what your circumstances look like.

I am El Shaddai ... the God who is more than enough. The more you believe, the more I will manifest My presence ... where I am troubles will flee ... darkness will leave ... demons will run.

Realize you are going through trials to fulfill My plans for you. No one escapes trials on this earth. You can choose how you react ... stiff necked and hard headed ... angry and frustrated ... or choose to believe in Me and My plan for you ... choose to have faith in spite of what you're going through.

Faith (in Me) will bring you out of troubles ... to a higher level or you can choose to stay where you are. I would that you choose faith.

Day 49

{Luke 10:19}

Be careful that you do not give the devil a foothold through worry, doubt or fear. These are open doors to demonic strongholds (loopholes). Remember the words of encouragement I have given you ... be anxious for nothing ... do not fear ... I will never leave you ... the battle belongs to Me ... if I am for you (and I am) who can be against you ... nothing shall by any means hurt you ... you have power over all the power of the enemy ... by My stripes you are healed (spirit, soul and body) ... no weapon formed against you will prosper ... I will never leave you or forsake you ... this sickness is not unto death ... He who is in you is greater than he who is in the world ... the just shall live by faith ... do not fear bad news (evil tidings) but trust in the Lord.

Just because man does not know what else to do in a situation, doesn't mean that I don't ... My ways are not your ways ... I am a miracle working God ... I will make a way out of no way. I healed men when I walked this earth and I am still healing today ... in fact, I am the same yesterday, today and forever. *Let God's word be true and every man a liar.*

I can heal with a word and it is My will and My great pleasure to do so. I will deliver you and the pestilence shall not come nigh your dwelling place. You must not only call those things that be not as though they are ... but you must also see this in the spirit, believe and receive those things as though they already are ... for (as soon as you do this) it is so in the spirit.

Truly, when you pray and believe ... it is already so , in the spirit ... speak it out loud ... see it in the spirit ... believe it in your heart for then you will see it manifest in the physical.

Day 50

{Romans 8:28}

My child, rest assured that My plans for you are for good and not evil. No one can stop the plan I have for you. Every event, every circumstance in your life has been carefully orchestrated ... planned to the last detail.

There is a purpose to everything. I said that the poor will be with you always ... this includes the poor in spirit and the poor in health. They will always be with you so there is always an opportunity to pray for each other and carry each other's burdens.

No one is meant to carry their burdens by themselves. You were made to need each other. Some will try to isolate themselves and wall off others in times of trial ... they will find that retreating from others only makes things worse ... makes the burdens unbearable. My will is that you stand united with your face turned towards Me lifting each other up in prayer.

When one cries ... all should feel it. When one rejoices ... all should be happy with him. Nothing is impossible to those who stand united.

In times of trial let your tears flow, let your heart cry out to Me. I already have someone praying for you. I

Bernadette Hanson

understand the language of tears ... every sound has significance.

I am deeply moved by each one that turns to Me in their trials. Comfort ... true comfort ... is only found in My presence ... not in drugs, alcohol or anger. Turn to Me and receive the comfort that only I can give.

Day 51

{Hebrews 5:8}

Know that My protection is with you wherever you go. That nothing shall by any means hurt you. Wherever I send you ... I send My protection ... I send My provision.

I will fully equip you before sending you out. You may not feel ready ... but if I send you ... you are.

My people will suffer persecution for My sake. They will suffer just because they believe in Me. But I will bring them joy, patience and peace in the midst of their suffering.

They will be able to turn to Me, to praise me, right in the middle of their suffering (Paul and Silas in jail). Because you will suffer with Me ... you will reign with Me.

Some things are only taught ... received ... recognized through suffering. You will learn to turn to Me first during times of trial. You will cry out, and I will hear and deliver you (like sheep bleating in distress and the shepherd comes to save them).

Did not Jesus learn obedience by suffering? Realize that suffering is only for this world ... when you come home, there is no sadness, no sickness, no disease, no more suffering ... a place of perfect peace in My presence.

I will give you hope and increase your faith ... for it is My will that none give up during the struggle. Trust Me.

Day 52

{Matthew 6:21}

*L*et us speak of worldly possessions ... truly these will pass away. Do not store up earthly goods, but heavenly goods ... for earthly goods will rust and rot away, but heavenly goods are forever.

There is a currency and an economy in heaven ... but you must use heavenly currency to purchase something in heaven. Yes, heaven is a city and it has heavenly goods for sale.

It is open daily for (purchases) for those in heaven and open for deposits from saints on earth.

Every time you proclaim My Gospel, every time you help the needy ... both financially and spiritually ... a deposit is made to your heavenly account. Some will be rich as soon as they enter heaven. Others will build up their heavenly account day by day when they get here. Some will not have any time to add to their account while still on earth because they will receive Me and My blood sacrifice on their death bed or their works will be burnt up (things done with the wrong attitude of the heart).

Be aware that your heavenly account can be added to on any given day ... so store up your treasures in heaven where they do not rot away.

Bernadette Hanson

Preach My Word, feed the hungry, help the widows and orphans, heal the sick, pray for those in need ... all these will add to your spiritual account.

As soon as you see what there is to spend on in the heavenlies (shop) ... you will greatly desire to increase your heavenly account ... Selah

Day 53

{Revelation 21:21}

*H*eaven is a place of wondrous things and supernatural beings. Yes, there are streets here that look like they're made of (pure) gold. There is a River of Life that flows through here and a tree with leaves for the healing of the nations.

There are many mansions and saints from all generations who gather for praise and for the reading of My Word. Even in heaven, there is daily teaching and reading of My Word.

There is daily communion in My presence. There is music here that is indescribable in your language. There is eternal light and great joy. Time flows in a different way here. Not only will you find saints here, but many types of angels and other spiritual beings.

My throne is in the center ... all light comes from My presence. There is no sadness, no sickness, no disease ... nothing that is corruptible is allowed in.

Jesus makes daily intercession for the saints still on earth ... proclaiming redemption through His blood sacrifice ... a payment made at great price ... once and for all ... for all sins. There is joy unspeakable and peace that passes understanding. Even here, each one has ministries done on a daily basis.

Here, one sees the things of the spirit clearly ... whereas on earth some of these mysteries are seen darkly ... not fully understood.

Entrance is gained through a relationship with My Son, Jesus, and not by works that any man should boast. No one will buy, barter, argue, bribe, manipulate or bully their way in.

It is a place of great wonders that the (natural) eye has not seen neither has the (natural) ear heard.

Day 54

{2 Chronicles 7:14}

My people must turn from the wicked ways of the world. Instead of gambling ... turn to Me for provision. Instead of liquor and drugs ... turn to me for comfort and assurance. Instead of fornication ... remember that you are My bride whether or not you have a spouse.

I am coming for a bride without spot or wrinkle, a bride worthy of the King of kings and Lord of lords. I would that you turn to me first for all of your needs.

The steps of the righteous man are ordered by the Lord. I open doors that no man can shut ... I shut doors that no man can open. I have a plan for your life ... if you would only follow My will. My yoke is easy and My burden is light. I will complete the good work I've begun in you.

If you would only take time to listen ... if you would only trust and believe ... I will work it out for your good. It may not look good at the time ... but believe Me ... My plan will go forth. You will only frustrate yourself when you take things into your own hands.

Just take time to pray, to fast, and to listen. Very few are fasting and this is what brings the flesh under control ... this breaks the bondage (yokes). This allows you to hear Me clearly.

Bernadette Hanson

You will go through trials, but I am always with you and I am always in control.

Day 55

{Psalms 23:5}

My child, listen and remember ... ponder My Word in your heart, for it gives life and brings changes to the situations you're facing. Do you want healing ... reach out for the hem of My garment ... this is where healing awaits you.

Speak those things that be not as though they are and the things that have been dead in your life will live again ... relationships ... finances ... health. Meditate on and continually (verbally) speak forth My Word. In it is life and every good blessing ... every provision ... protection from your enemies.

As long as you walk this earth you will have enemies, but I will set a table for you before your enemies. Just when your enemy thinks you are defeated, I will show them how I used them to bring about My blessing for you.

I have made some vessels unto honor and some dishonor. I know who will choose to receive Me. Yet I will let you endure trials to strengthen you, to draw you closer to Me, to reveal to you what is in your inner most heart.

As a mother watches over her children ... I am never far from My own. I know how much you can bear. As you endure more, you will reach higher (spiritual) levels and become closer to Me. The closer you are to Me ... the less the cares of this world affect you.

Reflect on the eternal things ... the things that do not perish ... when you begin to understand that, you will see what is visible and temporary for what it really is.

Day 56

{Mark 11:24}

Speak those things that be not as though they are ... speak to the things in your life that are dead to quicken them to life. Speak life into your spirit man ... speak life into your ministry and anointing ... speak life into your relationships (marriage/family) ... speak life into your physical body (remember Abraham and Sarah) ... speak life into your finances.

Strengthen your words of life ... water them with prayer, fasting and faith. When you have done all ... stand and believe with an unwavering faith regardless of how it looks in the physical (natural) realm. Do not let what you see with your physical eyes discourage you, for a double minded man cannot hope to receive anything ... so stand in faith with the eyes of the spirit ... when you do this, you can be sure that I am arranging things in the spirit.

Things will be accomplished in the spirit realm before they are allowed to manifest in the physical realm. In the world, you see something happen in the physical and then believe in the spirit ... if you are truly Mine you MUST walk by faith ... you must see with your spiritual eyes ... you must receive the moment you believe ... you must call those things that be not as though they already are.

Bernadette Hanson

Without faith it is impossible to please Me. These things move Me ... a contrite and broken spirit ... a child-like faith ... humility and reverence. Your tears and your cries do not move Me like your faith does. Miracles are born of faith.

Did I not say that faith moves mountains ... speak (out loud) to your mountains, then stand (like flint) steadfast in faith ... believing that the mountains will move, and watch Me move them for you ... Selah.

Day 57

{Matthew 18:21-22}

As much as it is possible, walk in peace with those around you. There is a time for righteous anger ... this is for changing a wrong (wrongful situation). Jesus showed righteous anger when He overturned the tables of the money changers in My temple.

My temple is a place of reverence ... a place of humble prayer. Agree quickly with your enemy ... forgive your enemies 70 x 7. Pray for those who despitefully use you and bless those that curse you. In this way, the battle becomes Mine ... and your enemies' curse against you and your family are broken.

If you forgive your enemies, I will make them walk in peace with you. When you make a habit of walking in forgiveness, you defeat the spirits of heaviness, depression and anger. If unforgiveness takes root in your heart, your physical body will suffer real physical ailments ... (headaches, ulcers, chest pain, and high blood pressure).

Walk in peace, walk in forgiveness ... then you will walk in health. Do not fret that forgiving your enemy absolves them of their offense towards you ... your forgiveness makes the battle Mine ... they will answer to Me. I am perfect justice ... love compels Me to judge with absolute fairness ... this is why I want you to forgive ... because if you don't, you too will be subject to My judgment and judgment begins in My house.

Walking in love will give you the understanding and compassion you need to forgive your enemies. If you walk in love you will see the world through My eyes ... you will see how your enemies strike out in their pain and despair ... you will have mercy on them.

Day 58

{Hebrews 13:5}

My child, you have weathered many storms ... I have been with you. You need to trust Me more ... to listen to Me more ... to immediately give all your cares and concerns to Me. Is there anything that is impossible for Me? I will not fail or forsake you.

My plans for you are to bring about a good and expected end, not evil. No matter what it looks like, I have it under control. Nothing happens unless I permit it.

As a parent is never far from a child learning to ride a bike or walk ... I am never far from you. Don't listen to the lies of the enemy ... just look at the fruit it produces ... confusion, hurt, anger, guilt, shame, and hatred ... these are not from Me ... choose My Word and My report.

You must choose and believe what My Word says before it manifests in the physical. Nothing is too hard for Me. I will fix the broken pieces of your life ... I will heal the hurts that no amount of medication can touch.

I am for you, I am with you, I am in you ... TRUST Me ... have faith ... I cannot lie. I love you so much that I willingly gave My life for you ... even before you chose to know Me. My plan for you has purpose, you were made specifically to fulfill your destiny.

Bernadette Hanson

Choose Me, trust Me, have faith in Me ... to truly know and follow Me is to have contentment and fulfillment.

Day 59

{Romans 12:21}

It's time to set your face like flint ... time to fix your heart (attitude) ... the enemy will not overcome My children, but evil will be overcome by good. Remember, that love is the strongest force on earth ... My love overcame all evil for all time.

Declare the power and the benefits of My love. I am for you ... and if I am for you, who can be against you? The enemy can only do what I allow ... and I will not allow My children to be tested to the point of breaking.

Take a stand ... set your mind ... set your face as flint ... for I am moving in the earth right now more than any other time in history. My miracles will become commonplace ... all the earth shall know of Me. Some will still not choose Me no matter what signs are given ... woe unto them.

My judgment is sure. The time of grace will come to an end for I will not strive with man forever. The laborer must work while it is yet day ... the harvest is great. Many, many souls are in the valley of decision ... where will they choose to spend eternity?

Hell is a real place ... devoid of all things good ... devoid of My presence. The horrors of Hell are unspeakable. The torment goes on both night and day. The souls of Hell cry out to be saved, but the choice they made while alive cannot be changed.

Imagine the pain and suffering of the souls there. They have chosen to reject the blood sacrifice made on the cross at Calvary. My heart weeps for them, but I will not overrule their free will.

Day 60

{Psalms 34:19}

My child, I see your struggles, I hear your cries, I feel your tears. Know that I am with you, I am for you, I am in you and this too shall pass. Many are the afflictions of the righteous, but the Lord shall deliver you from them ALL.

I will bless those that bless you and curse those that curse you, for you are My very own. Yet a little while and you will remember your sorrows no more. Trust Me in this ... miracles are here now, deliverance is here now.

The situations and circumstances that are distressing you right now ... they will pass. Didn't I say that times will come as a woman's labor pains ... more frequent, more painful ... but these will pass. I will have great mercy on My own (people). Dry your tears and take comfort in My presence.

I am for you ... I love you ... I will not forsake you. Speak to Me any time you need to be comforted. I do not slumber or sleep and I love to talk with My children. Remember that your time on earth is short ... eternity awaits.

The joys of heaven are indescribable ... there is no sorrow there. Eye has not seen nor has ear heard (I Corinthians 2:9) the joys of heaven. Cast your cares unto Me ... give Me your burdens. You must learn not to hold onto loads that are too heavy and not meant for you to carry alone.

Come to Me in your sorrow and I will give you comfort and rest.

BONUS DAY

{Isaiah 43:19}

Today the blessings of the Lord have been upon you and your household. Behold, I will do a new thing in your life ... get ready for a change.

Your heart has been crying out for a change ... for deliverance ... for restoration. I will move quickly ... times of great blessings are upon you. I will pour out My blessings from the very windows of heaven.

You will experience joy and contentment on earth, but this does not compare to the blessings you will experience in heaven. No language on earth can begin to describe the peace, the joy, and the wonders of heaven.

Now you see darkly ... in part ... but when you arrive in heaven, you will see fully (clearly). I see all things from beginning to end, which is why I can assure you that times of trials and testing are only temporary.

The race is not given to the swift, ... but to the one who endures to the end. You must run the race with faith no matter what it looks like. Do not be fooled by your emotions ... react with faith. I can and will change circumstances ... but it will be in My time. Be assured that I will not test you to the breaking point.

Bernadette Hanson

Stay close to Me ... I am here to guide and comfort you at all times. You need only call on Me, I am with you.

30 More Days with JESUS

Notes:

Bernadette Hanson's Bio

Bernadette Hanson is a Chicagoan who authored her debut Prophetic Devotional, "30 Days with Jesus". As you can see, she has added additional days in this second book of the series, "30 More Days With Jesus".

Bernadette will start touring this year in 2011, presenting her literary works. Her burden and passion for wounded women has threshed her into her ministry Beauty for Ashes.

She is an ordained Evangelist, a Psalmist/song writer, vocalist and loves to minister through teaching and speaking. Bernadette is currently involved in women's symposiums where she is committed to leading seminars and workshops.

As a mother and Grandmother, she still finds time to teach Sunday School and is active in various outreach ministries with her home church. Bernadette holds degrees in both Nursing and Psychology and is currently in training to be a Life Coach.

www.ingramcontent.com/pod-product-compliance
Lightning Source LLC
Chambersburg PA
CBHW031254290426
44109CB00012B/571